THE POWER OF Music

IN THE CHRISTIAN LIFE

BY PASTOR DOUG BATCHELOR

The Power of Music in the Christian Life
By Doug Batchelor

Copyright © 2021 by Doug Batchelor
All rights reserved. Printed in the USA.

Published by Amazing Facts International
P.O. Box 1058, Roseville, CA 95678-8058
amazingfacts.org | afbookstore.com

Unless otherwise noted, Scripture taken from the New King James Version ®. Copyright © 1982 by Thomas Nelson. Used by permission. All rights reserved.

Cover: Abby Osinjolu
Layout: Jacob McBlane

ISBN 978-1-95250-504-1

Table of Contents

Introduction 4

Be Careful What You Hear 13

Music, a Powerful Teacher 37

The Revolution of Music 50

Music in the Church 61

Introduction

"Be filled with the Spirit, speaking to one another in psalms and hymns and spiritual songs, singing and making melody in your heart to the Lord."
—Ephesians 5:18, 19

After decades of being brutalized by Nazi Germany and then the Soviet Union, citizens of the tiny nation of Estonia voiced their desire for independence in the best way they knew how: singing.

Under the USSR, Estonian national songs and hymns were forbidden, but as the yearning for freedom grew, the people began to publicly sing them as an act of defiance. These protests culminated at the "Song of Estonia" festival in 1988, where 300,000 people—over a quarter of the population—gathered to sing songs of independence.

The singing so strengthened national unity that the Soviets eventually rolled in tanks to destroy many of Estonia's radio and television towers. Ever vigilant, however, Estonian citizens formed human shields to stop the tanks. On August 20, 1991, thanks in part to the "singing revolution," Estonia gained its independence without any military action.

The Bible documents a similar amazing story about the people of Judah. A confederacy of three nations had formed for the purpose of annihilating Judah. Knowing that his people and armies were vastly outnumbered, King Jehoshaphat turned to the Lord and prayed for guidance. Under the inspiration of the Spirit, a prophet told the king what the Lord wanted His people to do:

Jehoshaphat … appointed those who should sing to the LORD, and who should praise the beauty of holiness, as they went out before the army and were saying: "Praise the LORD, for His mercy endures forever." Now when they began to sing and to praise, the LORD set ambushes against the people of Ammon, Moab, and Mount Seir, who had come against Judah; and they were defeated. For the people of Ammon and Moab stood up against the inhabitants of Mount Seir to utterly kill and destroy them. And when they had made an end of the inhabitants of Seir, they helped to destroy one another. So when Judah came to a place overlooking the wilderness, they looked toward the multitude; and there were their dead bodies, fallen on the earth. No one had escaped" (2 Chronicles 20:20–24).

God used music to deliver them—but not just any kind of music: joyful, spiritual songs, with authentic singing born from faith in the midst of a real crisis. Here we get a taste of just how powerful music can be in a believer's life.

INTRODUCTION

I believe the Creator hardwired our brains to tell the difference between music and noise. Music is more than a collection of random notes. And there's a reason for that. Music says a lot *to* us; however, equally important, the music we choose also says something *about* us.

There is no denying that different types of music have widely varying effects on people. The poignant violin strains of "Ashokan Farewell," a tune made popular by the PBS docuseries *Civil War*, can evoke strong emotions, even tears. On the other hand, listening to "The Stars & Stripes Forever" by John Philip Sousa is practically guaranteed to prod a patriotic hearer to his feet and set him off marching around the room.

Music can reach people's hearts, bodies, and emotions in potent ways as nothing else can. That's why it is important to be discerning and deliberate when selecting and listening to music, particularly if you are seeking to follow Jesus during these last days.

Music Choices "Speak" About Us

As I mentioned, the music we choose to listen to says something about our hearts.

I once arranged for a fellow Christian to pick me up at the airport. As we drove along, he said, "I want to catch the news," and then switched on his radio. But instead of a weather and traffic report, the first sounds that erupted from his car's speakers stunned me: It was screeching, wild music that, in my humble opinion, no Christian should listen to. (We'll unpack the "why" later.)

The driver quickly fiddled with the radio controls, until he realized the tune wasn't coming from a random radio station—it was from a CD! Evidently, to his great chagrin, he had forgotten it had been the last thing he'd been listening to before picking me up. My unspoken question for him was, "What's going on in your heart that this violent music is what you choose to listen to?"

Motivational speaker Charlie "Tremendous" Jones was famous for saying, "You will be the same person in five years as you are today except for the people you meet and the books you read." I would also add: "and the music you listen to."

It's sad to say, but much of what typically airs on the most popular music radio stations today can be a hair-raising experience, especially when contrasted with what the Bible says Christians ought to be thinking about. Yes—it's true that the older generation typically says that about the music of teens and young adults. As this book is published, however, the popular music aimed at today's youth is so explicit, so sensual, and so filled with violence and inappropriate behavior that it's difficult to find a comparable era in history.

And what does that mean for our society today and in the future if music can set the tone of the various settings in which we find ourselves, whether at home one evening, while working, or during a worship service? The right music can season the moment in the most beautiful way, but a poor selection can have an equally negative impact.

Consider a powerful example from 1992. Trooper Bill Davidson of the Texas Department of Public Safety was shot and killed during a traffic stop. His assailant, Ronald Ray Howard, said the violence-themed rap music he constantly played drove him to his crime. While the jury rejected that as a defense, Davidson's widow sued a record company over the alleged inspiration the music gave Howard, who was later executed for his crime.

Howard's trial attorney, Allen Tanner, recalled the criminal's circumstances:

> He grew up in the ghetto and disliked police, and these [rappers] were his heroes, … telling him if you're pulled over, just blast away. It affected him.[1]

The role of such suggestive music in the murder of Trooper Davidson is hardly the only instance of such a connection. But it illustrates the potential influence of music. It's impossible to say with certainty whether or not Howard would have killed the police officer in cold blood had the young man been listening to Bach instead of late rapper Tupac Shakur, himself a victim of fatal gun violence. But there's little doubt that the rap music in which Howard immersed himself had a negative influence on his decision-making.

In contrast, consider the highly successful Dr. Ben Carson, famous brain surgeon turned politician. Before retiring from medicine and entering public service, Carson was reported to have performed more than 300 surgeries a year, almost three times the average of neurosurgeons. Carson made it his practice to listen to classical music—Bach, Mozart, Vivaldi, Handel, etc.—during surgeries, reporting that it served to keep him calm.[2] "The operating room is like a sanctuary," Carson said. "When the residents came [to me] to learn pediatric neurosurgery, they knew they were also going to learn classical music."[3]

Making Right Choices

The purpose of this book is not to advocate for classical music or vilify punk or rap music, but rather to establish principles on the influence of music in order to help you be a more selective consumer of music with a focus on eternity. We'll look to David, whose musical skills helped soothe a troubled king; we'll delve into music as a form of communication; and we'll examine the hot-button issue of music in the church.

How can we be faithful stewards of our minds and guard the avenues to our soul in terms of what we hear, whether it's on our commute, at home, or at church? It's my prayer that this short but informative book will help you discover ways to select and use music biblically, to deepen your walk with the Lord, and to help you make choices that glorify Him.

After all, a satisfying Christian life *is* something to sing about!

—*Pastor Doug*

Chapter 1

Be Careful What You Hear

An Amazing Fact: *Researchers at the University of California at Berkeley studied the emotional reactions of 2,500 people to a range of music—from classical to jazz to marching bands and even heavy metal. The result? "The subjective experience of music across cultures can be mapped within at least 13 overarching feelings: amusement, joy, eroticism, beauty, relaxation, sadness, dreaminess, triumph, anxiety, scariness, annoyance, defiance, and feeling pumped up."*[4]

Why do we love music? John Powell, in his book *Why We Love Music*, gathered information on this topic for four years before putting his research into plain language to help us better understand how our bodies and brains respond to music.

He explains that our bodies contain "an internal pharmacy that dispenses various chemicals" into the bloodstream. Music has a big effect on this process, not only on our emotions but consequently on our mental activities and physical reactions—in other words, our behavior.

Consider a classic piece such as the oratorio *Messiah* by George Frideric Handel. Legend has it that King George II was so moved by the crescendo of the "Hallelujah" chorus that the monarch felt compelled to stand, beginning a customary practice that continues with audiences today.

Or how about this one? During the winter of early 1943, as the Nazis were bogged down in their efforts to capture Stalingrad, the Soviet secret police set up loudspeakers all over the city and drove vans through its streets, blaring out eerie tango music, an ominous ticking clock, and debilitating messages, like how a German soldier was dying every seven seconds. At the end of the musical piece, the attack would begin. By February of that same year, 91,000 beleaguered and demoralized German soldiers surrendered.[5] That tango was made into one powerful weapon of discouragement.

In an online article, Powell shared:

> Experiments have demonstrated that music is extremely effective at curing insomnia; that shoppers spend more money in stores playing classical music; and that communal singing helps humans to bond with each other by releasing oxytocin into our system—the same chemical we experience during sex or breast-feeding.[6]

It's even been shown that in both work and exercise, listening to music can make the physical and mental exertion more pleasant and even more efficient. Wow. That's a massive range of impact, from health to the economy to intimate relationships!

Is it no wonder that we love something so personal, so effective, so meaningful?

The Language of Music

It's a well-accepted fact that up to 93 percent of communication is nonverbal. The interpretation of a given message is based on 55 percent visual (like body language) and 38 percent vocal (such as tone of voice); only about 7 percent is verbal.[7] What does that mean in terms of music?

Music is a language all by itself and has the ability to communicate a message all on its own. In fact, it is all the more powerful in that it is, in a sense, a universal language. It transcends verbal comprehension. No matter in which part of the world you live, a mother who is rocking her child to sleep will have some version of a lullaby to sing to her baby. Films produced in America are frequently released in other countries, dubbed into respective languages; but notice, the film score is almost never changed when sent overseas—and why would it be? Tense squeaks for a horror film or triumphant brass for an action sequence need no translation.

Did you know that various trumpet sounds communicated different messages to the Israelites in the wilderness? God instructed Moses, "Make two silver trumpets for yourself; you shall make them of hammered work; you shall use them for calling the congregation and for directing the movement of the camps" (Numbers 10:2). Sometimes they were blown to "sound an alarm" (v. 9) for war; sometimes they were blown to express "gladness" (v. 10) or at ceremonies, like at the Feast of Trumpets (Leviticus 23:24). And all of these sounded different.

Did you know that a trumpet will also be sounded at the second coming of Christ? "For the trumpet will sound, and the dead will be raised incorruptible, and we shall be changed," declares 1 Corinthians 15:52. What kind of glorious note might be played at the resurrection of the dead? It will doubtless be one that all the righteous, regardless of culture or ethnicity or era in which they lived, will be able to understand.

The Power of Lyrics

Now, this is not to say that lyrics are not important. The written word can also comfort, inspire, instruct, enrage, motivate, humor, or calm a person; it can speak truth or tell lies. Imagine the powerful influence of putting lyrics and music together.

My wife Karen and I have friends who enjoy playing a game that has this rule: You cannot use your voice unless you say something through a song. It's a lot of fun, and makes you realize how much you can communicate through music.

Frank Sinatra's signature song was "My Way"—a beautiful composition, but the words are all about living life for yourself. Take this last stanza, for example:

For what is a man? What has he got?
If not himself, then he has naught;
To say the things he truly feels
And not the words of one who kneels.

Neither did the devil want to bend the knee to our Almighty God, but instead boasted, "I will ascend into heaven, I will exalt my throne above the stars of God; ... I will be like the Most High" (Isaiah 14:13, 14).

There are many catchy music pieces in Mozart's opera *The Magic Flute*, which was written more than 225 years ago. For most listeners, the tunes sound lilting and pleasant, even inviting. Those who don't know German, however, are often shocked to read the English translation of the lyrics, which dip more than a toe into the waters of spiritualism.

If music can lodge words and values deep into our subconscious thoughts, eventually giving way to expression, as we have seen, then isn't it important for a Christian to consider not only the tunes they are hearing but the lyrics too?

Although it is true that some simple melodies could go either way; not every lyric is necessarily subject to its accompaniment. Consider the familiar nursery rhyme "Twinkle, Twinkle, Little Star."

In elementary school, some creative friends of mine thought up some evil words to the benign melody and totally transformed the nature of the song.

I remember hearing a song years ago that was written and sung by Don McLean called "Vincent." It starts off with the words, "Starry, starry night." I'd listened to that song for years, mostly for its beautiful melody. But one day I discovered the tragic story behind the music. McLean had been reading a book about Vincent Van Gogh and was inspired to compose a song about how the painter took his own life. It's a sad and depressing topic for such a beautiful melody. I thought to myself that the music shouldn't be wasted, so I wrote my own Christian lyrics for the tune.

But that is not a rule of thumb across the board; not all melodies are so pliable. Be careful of attempting to modify lyrics to familiar tunes. Sometimes it can backfire. I once spoke with a pastor who told me about an embarrassing experience he had while honoring some female church members who worked in the local community services ministry. As they came forward, he had asked the pianist to play the accompaniment to "I'm in the Lord's Army." Unbeknownst to the pastor though, the song he had chosen was originally the tune for an old folk song, whose lyrics went like this: "The old gray mare, she ain't what she used to be." It was, needless to say, quite an unfortunate choice for the many elderly women present.

What if you put wholesome lyrics to a violent tune? Would that make the entire piece good? What if I penned a psalm to a heavy metal number? Would your thoughts be turned to the humility of Christ as He lay His life upon the cross or the majesty of His resurrection in the quiet morning hours?

Good lyrics do not cancel out a bad melody, and vice versa. The music and lyrics work together, and they each hold weight in influence and impact. So, keep in mind that selecting good tunes requires discernment and commitment to following godly principles.

Music, Mood & Medicine

Perhaps you've heard of the "Mozart effect." One interesting study reveals how just one type of music can enhance your IQ. This Harvard health article states:

> The most highly publicized mental influence of music is the "Mozart effect." Struck by the observation that many musicians have unusual mathematical ability, researchers at the University of California, Irvine, investigated how listening to music affects cognitive function in general, and spatial-temporal reasoning in particular. In their first study, they administered standard IQ test questions to three groups of college students, comparing those who had spent 10 minutes listening to a Mozart piano sonata with a group that had been listening to a relaxation tape and one that had been waiting in silence. Mozart was the winner, consistently boosting test scores. Next, the investigators checked to see if the effect was specific to classical music or if any form of music would enhance mental performance. They compared Mozart's music with repetitive music by Philip Glass; again, Mozart

seemed to help, improving spatial reasoning as measured by complex paper cutting and folding tasks and short-term memory as measured by a 16-item test.[8]

The article also shows how certain music without words can lower stress, help with depression, improve stroke recovery, and help heart attack patients recover.

A 2015 review in medical journal *The Lancet* found that people who listened to music before, during, or after surgery experienced less pain and anxiety, compared to patients who did not listen to music. The music listeners didn't even need as much pain medication.[9]

One study conducted at the University of Pavia in Italy showed that music promotes a healthy cardiovascular system by "directly [triggering] physiological changes that modulate blood pressure, heart rate and respiration."[10] Researchers also found that "rich" classical music phrases, lasting 10 seconds long, "caused heart rate and other parts of the cardiovascular system to synchronize with the music."

It was not the only study to do so. In an online article called "How Music Can Influence the Body: Perspectives from Current Research" by Imogen Nicola Clark and Jeanette Tamplin, the authors explain:

> Musical tempo, harmony, melody, rhythm and volume in music can therefore be manipulated to regulate heart rate, blood pressure, sensory perception, cognitive function, neural activity, and emotional response depending on the requirements for a given situation.[11]

Most people intrinsically know that music has a profound effect on our moods. Have you ever called a business and been put on hold? Of course you have. What kind of music do they play while you're waiting? Something soothing is purposefully played, calculated to keep most people, who might otherwise become more irritable while endlessly parked on the phone, calm. Do you know why "elevator music" was invented? Nobody wants to panic in an elevator.

I was recently put on hold while waiting to talk with a pharmacist. They played calm, lilting guitar music. No business would dream of playing heavy metal at a time like that.

In 2013, *The Journal of Positive Psychology* put out a study that reported deliberate improvement of mood based on the type of music listened to. Participants became happier when listening to the compositions of Aaron Copland, known for invoking the pioneer spirit of America, rather than Igor Stravinsky's melancholic works.[12]

As you might expect, a happier mood brings benefits beyond feeling good. In a press release, lead study author Yuna Ferguson noted that happiness has been linked to "better physical health, higher income and greater relationship satisfaction."[13]

There's now even a segment of medicine called "music therapy." The American Music Therapy

Association (AMTA) reported that music therapy programs can be designed to achieve goals such as managing stress, enhancing memory, and alleviating pain. They have successfully assisted autistic children to those suffering from brain damage due to a stroke or Alzheimer's disease. They are used in palliative care in hospices, to ease the loneliness in nursing homes, as motivation in physical rehabilitation. Patients even may be assigned to write their own songs.

It's fascinating that a person who may struggle with stuttering finds it easier to sing words than to speak them.[14] I've seen this firsthand. It's amazing that people in senior centers struggling with dementia suddenly become more lucid when a group of children visit and begin to sing a familiar song, and that they often start to sing along, tapping their fingers in time. That's because music is a powerful way of storing memories.

According to one blog, "Therapists use a style of singing with certain rhythms that can help bring back the cadence of speech. The right side of the brain processes music while the left side processes language, so music therapy can help bridge the gap between the two. Music helps to create new neurological pathways."[15]

What do you think happens when you combine the power of the Word of God with restorative kinds of tunes? You'd get a double-barreled blast of communication that can heal the mind and body: "Is anyone cheerful? Let him sing psalms" (James 5:13). This is, indeed, exactly what happened between Saul and David. But what is truly amazing is that the Bible recounted a model of this music therapy ages before any of this modern research was ever completed.

The King's Music

Saul, the first king of Israel, had transformed into a deeply disturbed man. Originally chosen by God to rule over His people, Saul began his tenure as king with humility and a passion for obeying God. But after several years of successful battles, the king became proud and careless about following God's commandments. Eventually, the prophet Samuel told Saul that the Lord was choosing someone else to lead the nation.

Soon after, Samuel was sent to anoint that next leader, David, a young man who had a heart filled with love for God. The Bible tells us, "Samuel took the horn of oil and anointed [David] in the midst of his brothers; and the Spirit of the LORD came upon David from that day forward" (1 Samuel 16:13).

Meanwhile Saul, brooding with jealousy, gradually became rash, despondent, and paranoid. Notice in the very next verse, it explains that *after* the Holy Spirit came upon David, "the Spirit of the LORD departed from Saul and a distressing spirit from the LORD troubled him" (v. 14). That same Holy Spirit that had left Saul now filled David. Note that the phrase "from the LORD" does not mean that God sent a demon to possess the king. It simply means that God did not prevent the devil from filling the void that His Spirit left.

Saul's poor frame of mind didn't go unnoticed by those around him. His servants could see that the king was mentally tormented. They witnessed him go through fits of rage and then sink into melancholic spells. Finally, someone spoke up:

> Then one of his servants answered and said, "Look, I have seen a son of Jesse the Bethlehemite, who is skillful in playing, a mighty man of valor, a man of war, prudent in speech, and a handsome person; and the LORD is with him" (v. 18).

In short, Saul needed to find someone to help him with his mental distress. Instead of calling for a wise counselor, they summoned a gifted singer and musician. Out of all the people in the kingdom who might have been called to assist the king, guess who gets invited to the palace? The very one who would soon take the king's place.

God's providence is uncanny—isn't it? I imagine that David entered Saul's court with some trepidation. He must have been extremely cautious about choosing his words and body language, knowing the volatile nature of the king, all while being aware that God had anointed him as the king's replacement.

A Gifted Musician

Abraham Lincoln, who underwent less than a year of formal education in his entire life, eventually became president of what would someday be the most powerful nation in the world. While no college graduate, he was a renowned bibliophile, borrowing and reading every book he could get his hands on. His favorites were the Bible and the works of William Shakespeare. This habit gave him that broad grasp of language seen in the Gettysburg address, the president's famous speech given in 1863, near the end of America's Civil War.

The Bible says that David was not only a man of war but also eloquent in speech. We don't usually think of a shepherd as a wordsmith, but David, like Lincoln, was a singular lad who rose to prominence in the government of his people. Just read the many psalms of David and you'll quickly agree that he was a gifted poet with a tremendous vernacular.

"So David came to Saul and stood before him. And he [Saul] loved him greatly" (v. 21); the king listened to the shepherd speak and recognized that David was a prudent, capable individual with great potential.

And could he ever play music! After the interview and audition, Saul sent a message back to Jesse: "Please let David stand before me, for he has found favor in my sight" (v. 22). Verse 23 continues,

> And so it was, whenever the spirit from God was upon Saul, that David would take a harp and play it with his hand. Then Saul would become refreshed and well, and the distressing spirit would depart from him.

David's music kept Saul's volatile temper at bay and broke the clouds of depression. Indeed, the songs of "the sweet psalmist of Israel" (2 Samuel 23:1) probably saved David's life and the lives of others during the years when Israel's first king was a target of demonic harassment.

Music Is Magnetic

"Playing loud pop songs has been proven as one of the most effective ways of fending off attackers," claimed the British Association of Private Security Companies.[16]

British naval officers apparently got the idea from U.S. armed forces, which had used music against rioters. The tactic has been largely successful against Somali pirates, especially, according to some reports, with the stylings of pop icon Britney Spears. "They're so effective the ship's security rarely needs to resort to firing guns," said one officer.

While in no way comparing the shepherd's heavenly music to contemporary pop, we see that David's music likewise helped to drive away evil spirits.

In fact, if there is godly music that has the power to push back the devil, is it a stretch to believe that there's also music that *invites* in evil spirits? If certain genres and rhythms can be so beneficial to our health, does it not follow that other types could be detrimental?

Yet many believe that all music is neutral, that there is no such thing as good or bad music. Their attitude is, "Whatever feels good to you is okay." I respectfully disagree. I believe music is like theology. Even without words, music can communicate a particular message just as much as the words you're reading in this book.

Read this inspiring statement:

As our Redeemer leads us to the threshold of the infinite, flush with the glory of God, we may catch the themes of praise and thanksgiving from the heavenly choir round about the throne. And as the echoes of the angels' song is awakened in our earthly homes, hearts will be drawn closer to the heavenly singers. Heaven's communion begins on earth where we learn here the keynote of its praise.[17]

Many times while sitting on the platform waiting to preach, I have observed people moved to tears by the words of some hymn or other beautifully presented music selection. The song may have been written over a century ago, but it is still able to touch the heart just as powerfully. The Christian experience is ever current because it speaks of eternal truths from our living God, who is "from everlasting to everlasting" (Psalm 90:2).

Now contrast this with the following experience: I grew up listening to the music of the world. I saw what it did to me, and I see what it still can do to me. Before I was a Christian, I occasionally attended rock concerts. I remember hearing the music accelerate and watching the audience get worked up into a frenzy; they began behaving like animals. I recall more than one berserk person running up to me out of their minds. Looking back now, they may have even been demon-possessed.

Do these two experiences sound neutral to you? It seems to me that they could not be more different.

Listen *Carefully*

Some of the music of the world is potent, exceedingly enticing to our carnal natures. And I'd be lying if I said I never find any of it attractive. Sometimes I do.

We are fooling ourselves if we do not think it affects us spiritually. Your spiritual health is not off limits to the devil. In fact, it is his special target. And how the devil attacks is by cunning, by wiles.

Why do you think music is so ubiquitous in our culture? The devil can use this bait effectively! Just think of all the different strings music can pull in our heart.

Look at it this way: While we don't feel the gravity of the moon, it's still enough to move the tides of the world. Because we don't feel it, does it mean that gravity does not exist? Of course not. Just because you don't feel the music influencing you spiritually, it does not mean that it isn't. On the contrary, knowing this principle should cause Christians to be selective in what they listen to. We need to remember that just because we like the sound of some music, it doesn't mean it's good for us spiritually.

Yet the sad thing is that many Christians don't even stop to think how their choice of music can lower their defenses to temptation—and welcome the devil in.

There's a song you might have heard as a child:

Oh, be careful, little ears, what you hear.
Oh, be careful, little ears, what you hear.
There's a Father up above, and He's
 looking down in love.
So, be careful, little ears, what you hear.

How many of us have forgotten that lesson? We need to be careful regarding what we hear, because music can reach us in ways almost nothing else can. So, *be careful, little*—or big—*ears, what you hear!*

Chapter 2

Music, a Powerful Teacher

An Amazing Fact: *"There are few things that stimulate the brain the way music does," an online Johns Hopkins' article quoted one otolaryngologist as saying. "If you want to keep your brain engaged throughout the aging process, listening to or playing music is a great tool. It provides a total brain workout."*[18]

Music can be an effective teacher in sealing deep spiritual insights into our memories.

The apostle Paul repeatedly instructed believers to share "psalms and hymns and spiritual songs, singing and making melody in your heart to the

Lord" (Ephesians 5:19). "Let the word of Christ dwell in you richly in all wisdom, teaching and admonishing one another in psalms and hymns and spiritual songs, singing with grace in your hearts to the Lord" (Colossians 3:16), he encouraged. Music is meant to be a tool for teaching spiritual truths.

What's the difference between psalms and hymns and spiritual songs? One music instructor identified it this way: Psalms are passages of the Bible set to music, typically from, as one might expect, the book of Psalms. Hymns are songs about God or one of His attributes. They could be about the Bible, such as "Give Me the Bible," or a biblical theme, such as "Great Is Thy Faithfulness." Spiritual songs are more personal songs about an individual's relationship with God.

The Purpose of Music

Whenever Johann Sebastian Bach finished composing a piece of music, he wrote "SDG" at the bottom of the page, short for *Soli Deo Gloria*, a Latin phrase meaning "for the glory of God alone." He intended for his music to point listeners to God—not himself or any other person.

The Bible indicates that the primary purpose of music is to praise God. References in the Bible reveal that the music of heaven is used almost exclusively for exalting God.

Found in the very heart of your Bible are 150 psalms, about half of which were written by David. In my study of them, I've noticed that the most common sentiment found is: "Praise the Lord!" Over and over again, David sings words of praise:

- "While I live I will praise the LORD; I will sing praises to my God while I have my being" (Psalm 146:2).
- "I will greatly praise the LORD with my mouth" (109:30).
- "With my song I will praise Him" (28:7).
- "Let heaven and earth praise Him" (69:34).
- "Praise Him for His mighty acts; praise Him according to His excellent greatness!" (150:2).

David did not limit His praise to God by only writing lyrics. Psalm 71:22, 23 say, "Also with the lute I will praise You—and Your faithfulness, O my God! To You I will sing with the harp."

Clearly one of the primary functions of music is to glorify God! Given our purpose for existence, that shouldn't surprise you. We were created to "give to the LORD the glory due His name" (96:8). In the kingdom of heaven, music plays a central role in uplifting our Creator. At the very Creation of our world, Scripture reveals that "the morning stars sang together, and all the sons of God shouted for joy" (Job 38:7). In the apostle John's apocalyptic vision, the inhabitants of heaven sing praises to Jesus Christ, "You are worthy to take the scroll, and to open its seals; for You were slain, and have redeemed us to God by Your blood" (Revelation 5:9).

Confucius once said, "If one should desire to know whether a kingdom is well governed, or if its morals are good or bad, the quality of its music will furnish the answer." You can tell something about a nation's health by the music its people are listening to.

The Scottish writer and politician Andrew Fletcher likewise said, "I knew a very wise man ... [who] believed that if a man were permitted to make all the ballads, he need not care who should make the laws of a nation." In other words, if someone could control the nation's music, he could control the minds of the people.

When we primarily focus our music on praising God, we invite the Creator to be the King of our minds and hearts; we acknowledge Him as the Supreme Ruler of our lives. We allow the Holy Spirit to heal our sinful souls and to transform us into God's image of love.

Learning Without Reading

In South Korea, scientists from the National Institute of Agricultural Biotechnology studied the effect of music on, of all things, plants. Among the 14 songs used, all in the classical genre, was Beethoven's "Moonlight Sonata." In the rice fields that were tested, the crops were found to grow quicker in certain sound waves, causing researchers to conclude that plants may possess genes that, in a way, render them able to "hear."

In centuries past, many of the common public were illiterate. In addition, hymnals were not easy to come by; they were pricey. We see them lining the backs of pews today, but even as late as the 18th century, churches did not have them readily available for every member. It was much the same with the Bible.

Singing provided a simple solution. Does not Scripture tell us, "Faith comes by hearing, and hearing by the word of God" (Romans 10:17)? While not everyone in a given church is at the same educational level or has had the same life experiences, just about everyone can appreciate music. You can, in a few verses, teach doctrine almost as effectively as an hour-long sermon. Now, I'm not saying we don't need sermons—but you can pack a lot of biblical truth into a half-dozen stanzas. Sing it on a regular basis over the course of months or years, and those truths will be lodged in your mind and easily recalled when the situation calls for it.

This was very much the case with William Booth and the early days of his missionary movement, known today by its familiar moniker the Salvation Army. Booth's mission field began in one of the roughest communities in England. Home to abject poverty, alcoholism, spousal abuse, child abuse, prostitution, and other horrors, East London was a hotbed of vice. The men and women who came to Booth's meetings were poorly educated, if at all. Many couldn't read. But what they did know were the popular pub songs of the time.

So, Booth and his lieutenants tried a controversial tactic, fitting doctrine-packed verses to the melodies of those barroom ballads. Every meeting featured a good number of such songs; brass bands marched through the streets playing the familiar tunes—with the result that crowds were drawn to hear the gospel! The music met the people where they were and then elevated them to heavenly thoughts. This is what Booth had to say about his own method:

I rather enjoy robbing the devil of his choicest tunes, and, after his subjects themselves, music is about the best commodity he possesses. It is like taking the enemy's guns and turning them against him.[19]

Note that this was one situation where the music was able to be conformed to the meaning of the lyrics, and that it was done with discernment and intention. I do not think the same could be done with today's nightclub playlist.

Music as a Witness

For the better part of 50 years, Johnny Barnes, an electrician and bus driver in Hamilton, Bermuda, would stand daily at a roundabout intersection and wave at drivers, saying, "I love you" and "God loves you." He was so noted for his witness that the island erected a statue in his honor. When he died in 2016, schoolchildren lined the street for his funeral procession and the country's prime minister praised his example.

Barnes witnessed to the people of Bermuda in a simple yet powerful manner. In much the same way, your choice of music—whether at home, work, church, or even on a street corner—can be a heavenly witness to others, even when you think nobody else is listening.

When I rent a car while traveling, it's not uncommon for me to find music left by the previous occupant that would invite the devil to be my passenger. More than once, I've actually pulled the car over to change radio stations before continuing my journey.

So, before returning my rental, I make it a point to find as many Christian and classical stations and make them the preset stations on the car radio. Maybe the next driver will hear something that will inspire him to consider Christianity. Perhaps the attendant, while checking in the car, will hear a snippet that may lead him to study the Bible. I want to be a witness for Christ wherever I go; and God has a thousand ways to reach people—this could be one of them.

Look at David. His objective was to use his music as a witness to the world. Psalm 57, written when the former shepherd was on the run from Saul, says, "I will praise You, O Lord, among the peoples; I will sing to You among the nations" (v. 9).

After all, teaching others about God is what witnessing is all about—and music is a tool designed to do just that.

A New Song

Don't let your song list go stale. I believe that God is also pleased when His people keep the music fresh by occasionally introducing a new song. David even wrote, "Oh, sing to the Lord a new song! Sing to the Lord, all the earth" (96:1).

Because so much of the new music compromises on biblical principles, some automatically assume any new song must be bad. But every song you sing was at one time or another a new song.

And sometimes an old song can be a new song for you if it's the first time you hear it. When I first joined the church and began singing out of the hymnal, I fell in love with a number of the "old songs." People wondered why I was so excited about some of these old hymns. Well, they were brand new to me! I always appreciate a song service or a sing-along with friends where I learn a good, new song. Then I typically wear that song out, singing it until it becomes part of my internal catalogue.

God created us to appreciate variety and discover new things. Do you think we won't be learning new songs in heaven? Indeed, we will be singing about things that haven't even happened yet, like God's most glorious, culminating act of redemption when He comes to take us home. That will certainly be something new for which to sing praises to our God.

The Bible tells us that when these events are to come—Jesus Christ's second coming, the final judgment, the creation of the new heaven and the new earth, to name a few—that when we see our Lord and Savior face to face, when we understand fully what He has done for us and what He will have done for us, laudations will burst forth from our lips:

"They sang as it were a new song before the throne" (Revelation 14:3). "Blessing and honor and glory and power be to Him who sits on the throne, and to the Lamb, forever and ever!" (5:13) we all will sing.

In the 19th century, Johnson Oatman Jr. discovered that he had a musical gift to write hymns. Some believe he composed about 5,000 songs during his 66 years. To help you understand the depth of Oatman's commitment to uplifting Christ, he once wrote this dedication in a book: "Let others sing of rights or wrongs, sing anything that pleases; but while they're singing other songs, I'll sing a song for Jesus."[20]

I close this chapter with the words of one of his most famous hymns, "Holy, Holy, Is What the Angels Sing," written in 1894, a reminder that someday we will sing with angels in heaven.

> There is singing up in Heaven, such
>   as we have never known,
> Where the angels sing the praises of
>   the Lamb upon the throne.

> Their sweet harps are ever tuneful
>   and their voices always clear.
> O that we might be more like them
>   while we serve the Master here!
>
> Holy, holy, is what the angels sing,
> And I expect to help them make
>   the courts of Heaven ring;
> But when I sing redemption's story,
>   they will fold their wings,
> For angels never felt the joys that
>   our salvation brings.

I love this hymn; it reminds me that someday we'll have the privilege of worshiping God and singing in person. But more than that, there is salvation music that we'll sing based on our own experience of receiving Christ and being delivered from sin.

But if we would sing with angels in heaven, we must first learn to sing about our redemption here on the earth.

Chapter 3

The Revolution of Music

An Amazing Fact: *A childhood accident left him hard of hearing, and an elementary school teacher dubbed him "slow" and unlikely to learn. Yet by the end of his life, Thomas Alva Edison had invented the electric light bulb, improved the telephone and the telegraph, and accumulated more patents than any other American. But it was his 1877 invention of the phonograph that would change music forever. Although Edison thought his device could make children's dolls "speak" as well as preserve "the last words of dying persons," he admitted, "The phonograph will undoubtedly be liberally devoted to music."*[21]

Strange as it may seem, recorded music is a relatively recent phenomenon. Before Edison introduced the phonograph, music was consumed much differently. Let's take a look at a cursory history of music.

The first reference to a musician and musical instruments in the Bible is Jubal, the son of Lamech, seventh generation after Adam through Cain. Of this pre-Flood man, Genesis says that "[he] was the father of all those who play the harp and the flute" (4:21) and might well have been the inventor of those instruments. The Hebrew name *Jubal* means "joyful sound," though some associate the name to a ram's horn. It is also connected to the words "Jubilee" and "jubilation."

Did you know that God sings (Zephaniah 3:17)? Even before manmade instruments, God made man's first instrument, the human voice—and there is none that can equal it. There are a million different animal voices on Earth, but none is as versatile as the human voice.

When we speak,

"72 sets of muscles work with split-second timing. In talking for one minute, the tongue, jaw, and lips make at least 300 separate movements. At the same time, our vocal cords are vibrating and … our respiratory muscles … [forcing] out just the right amount of air. And if this isn't complex enough, think of the many inflections the voice is capable of making, ranging up to nearly 500 audible pitches. One can vary the tone tremendously from a shout to a delicate whisper.[22]

To sing, we depend on two small bands of muscle tissue called "vocal cords" that vibrate to produce sound. The higher the note, the faster the speed of vibrations. For example, a high C takes 1,200 vibrations per second. If you've ever listened to an acapella group, you can hear the incredible beauty that can be found in the human voice alone.

It was only in the 10th century ad that Christians began to have instrumental accompaniment during divine service.[23] Up until then, believers would sing without the aid of the organ or piano or anything else. The organ, though now familiarly associated with churches, began as a feature in secular attractions, like at the games of Ancient Rome.[24]

And all of this was always ever done live. Indeed, the majority of human existence had no recorded music. Music was a skill to be refined. Scales were painstakingly practiced day after day; the ear was fine-tuned to the concise pitch. And people longed for an opportunity to hear their favorite piece. But if you wanted to listen to music, you heard a live performance by an orchestra, a soloist, a choir, or grandpa playing his fiddle—or you did it yourself. There was no other option.

But after the invention of the phonograph, a seismic cultural transformation took place, with consequences that have profoundly influenced our world.

Music Saturation

In just a little more than a century and a half, there has been an explosion of hyper-access to music

24/7—the phonograph's wax cylinders, then record players, then tape players, CDs, DVDs, MP3 players, and now livestreaming on the Internet. Listening to a beautiful piece of music is no longer something you have to wait months to hear or purchase tickets to experience.

The music industry was created to make money by selling music. In an industry worth more than $20 billion, over half the revenues come from digital streaming. In 2018, hip-hop/rap accounted for almost 22 percent of the music album market, with pop (20 percent), rock (14 percent), and R&B (11 percent) close behind. Incidentally, the religious genre made up only 3 percent of the market.[25]

In order to succeed in this type of industry, musicians are constantly having to create something new, something that pushes the envelope. High-tech studios and powerful software programs can now make sounds that are out of this world. They can remove all the "blemishes" from a performance, enhancing singers' voices beyond their normal abilities, making everything in perfect time and tune.

They can even synthesize the accompaniment so that real instruments are not needed.

But this also means that music is often created to appeal to people's lusts, to give them what they want so that they'll keep on buying and buying, and listening and listening, and craving and never able to stop. After all, $20 billion is nothing to sneeze at.

Music is now omnipresent, available at our fingertips through smartphones, through an instantaneous click of a button. You hear it from the time you wake up in the morning until you crash in bed at night. Music is in our cars, in restaurants, gyms, grocery stores, malls, movies, at our work, at church, and even at our bedsides as we drift off to sleep at night. We're living in a time when, in theory, you could be listening to a different song for every hour of your day for the rest of your life and never hear the same song twice!

How Much Is Too Much?

In the 1700s, the average consumption of sugar in the developed world was approximately 4 pounds annually and accounted for less than 1 percent of calorie intake. By 1800, this had risen to approximately 18 pounds; by 1900, it was 60 pounds. In 2009, 50 percent of Americans consumed approximately 227 grams of sugar each day—equating to 178 pounds a year!

The human body needs glucose to survive, of course. But having too much sugar—especially refined sugar—will lead to a long list of health problems: "Have you found honey? Eat only as much as you need, lest you be filled with it and vomit" (Proverbs 25:16). So, can a person listen to too much music?

Like sugar, too much music can be bad for you. And the issue lies in the pervasiveness of the types of music that don't feed the soul. Just going about my day, I can't help but hear plenty of it. For instance, I enjoy going to a local Mexican restaurant for a good vegetarian burrito every now and then. Great food, sure, but the problem is that sometimes the background music in that restaurant is worldly—and loud enough to not be able to ignore it. More than once, I've gone to the counter and asked, "Can you please turn the music down a little? It is difficult to have a conversation at my table." Sometimes I get a phone call while I'm there, and the caller, hearing the wild noise in the background, will ask, "Where in the world are you?"

I admit that I get a little self-conscious in those moments, and I'll say to the caller, "Sorry. I'm in a restaurant." But it really could be anywhere—because it is everywhere you go. The simple fact is that in public places, we're often surrounded by the music that's popular in the culture.

You might find it surprising that the World Health Organization, concerned about premature hearing loss in young adults, recommends that people do not listen to music more than one hour a day—and not past a certain volume either.[26] But it's not just a concern about hearing loss. The auditory nerves in our brains need rest like everything else.

Many of us take it for granted, but hearing is an amazing and intricate five-part process:

1. Sounds are waves in the environment around us. The outer ear gets these waves and transports them down a tube, called the ear canal, to a delicate, flat plate, called the eardrum.
2. The sound waves then reach the eardrum, causing it to vibrate. The vibration subsequently transfers to the middle ear, in which are three tiny bones.
3. The movement of the three tiny bones transfers to the inner ear, in which there is fluid.
4. The movement of the fluid transfers to the cochlea, a snail-shaped organ also in the inner ear. The cochlea has tiny hair cells, which bend at the movement of the fluid, changing it into electrochemical signals.
5. The signals are then sent through the cochlear nerve, which get them to the brain, which precisely interprets them as a broad spectrum of various sounds.[27]

Each of your ears performs this complicated function for every sound it hears! We brush our teeth because we want them to last a lifetime; should we also not care for our ears just as diligently?

What else might we lose with this plethora of music? Do songs that once brought you happiness or comfort now sound stale and boring because you "played them out"? I remember when you'd listen to the radio for a favorite artist or a favorite tune, and when it would come on, you'd turn up the volume and enjoy the special moment of hearing it. You may not hear that song again for days or weeks! Are we just sucking all the spontaneity out of simple pleasures?

Ultimately, this all begs the question: What are you *not* listening to when you're playing that constant soundtrack in your ears?

The Lord says, "Be still, and know that I am God" (Psalm 46:10). What happens to that "still small voice" (1 Kings 19:12) when we have other sounds competing with Him? Or what happens when those other sounds begin to tune Him out, even without our realizing? It is not that God cannot be thunderously loud (Psalm 29:3, 4), but what if He chooses not to be? What if there is a reason why He is not? What does it do to our minds to have peace and quiet? Sometimes, we can best hear the voice of God in silence.

If we want to follow Jesus and live for Him, we'll keep our hearts and minds in a condition that will reflect His desires for us. If you were to ask Jesus to walk through your home and help you clean out everything that didn't reflect heaven's best for your life, what would happen if He browsed through your music? Would He suggest you toss some of the tunes that you think are harmless—or even some you think are good?

Today, with ready access to millions of songs at our fingertips, we need God's help more than ever to guard our hearts from shallow music that takes our minds away from heavenly principles. Let's swap out ungodly tunes with music that glorifies God and teaches the truths we need in these last days.

Chapter 4

Music in the Church

An Amazing Fact: *John Huss was a forerunner of the Protestant Reformation, and his works had deep repercussions on the father of it, Martin Luther. Like many of the Reformers who would come after him, Huss was, on July 6, 1415, sentenced to execution by the Catholic Church. While being burned at the stake, he began to sing hymns—and a miracle took place, for "scarce could the vehemency of the fire stop [his] singing."*[28]

Historians recount the same miracle occurring at the execution of Huss' closest associate, Jerome. "What fear, what vehement desire, what zeal, what vindication!" (2 Corinthians 7:11) to quote the apostle Paul. These were men who, while being tortured to death in a most inhumane fashion, were singing joyful praises to God. At their deaths was the culminating demonstration of their faith—and they chose to illustrate it in song.

What does our music mean to us Christians today? Are we using our music to glorify God, or is our music using us?

Christian Music Instructs

Leonard Warren was a popular singer with New York's Metropolitan Opera. On March 4, 1960, he was performing in the opera *La Forza del Destino* as the character Don Carlo, whose aria in Act III opens with the words: "To die, a momentous thing." As Warren sang that very song, tragically, ironically, he fell over and died. Only 48 years old at the time, he is believed to have died of a heart attack.

One Christian commentator said, "Talk unbelief, and you will have unbelief; but talk faith, and you will have faith. According to the seed sown will be the harvest."[29] Have we been singing faith or singing unbelief? The answer is a good indication of how we have been living.

Christian songwriter Keith Getty illustrates this well:

> Let me start with something theologian John Stott once pointed out. In the 21st century, there are more Christians in more countries than ever before. Yet the average Christian in the world knows less about the Bible than the average secularist in the West did in the 1950s.

Getty then posits the *why*.

> During that time, children sang hymns in school assemblies and had religious instruction in schools. Those things, added to the nominal churchgoing that took place, meant the average non-Christian in the 1950s knew more Bible stories and Christian doctrine than the average evangelical today.

He then puts his finger on the importance of music.

Stott believed the way to help Christians flourish in the 21st century is to build deep believers. If we want to survive, never mind thrive, in this century, we have to build deep believers in the church. And throughout history, that has been done in part by congregational singing.[30]

Stott makes a good point. If music is a masterful teaching tool—and we have learned that it is—then why have Christians been taking advantage of it less and less to teach Bible truths in our churches?

Martin Luther understood the importance of music in communicating Scripture. Before the Protestant Reformation, church members did not sing in church; they listened to monks chant in Latin. Of course, hardly anyone knew what the monks were singing, though the music was certainly beautiful.

Giving his church members a choice to sing in Latin or in their native tongue, Luther quickly discovered that attendance dropped when people couldn't understand the words but soared when they could. When Luther realized the psalms were written in this manner, in Hebrew, the language of the Israelite people, he was prompted to write new hymns in the local German vernacular. He said, "Next to the Word of God, music deserves the highest praise. The gift of language combined with the gift of song was given to man that he should proclaim the Word of God through Music."

A Mighty Message

One of Luther's most influential hymns is "A Mighty Fortress," inspired by the Reformer's love of Psalm 46. Have you ever carefully read the words to this powerful song?

> A mighty fortress is our God, a
> > bulwark never failing.
> Our Helper He amid the flood of
> > mortal ills prevailing.
> For still our ancient foe doth
> > seek to work us woe.
> His craft and pow'r are great, and,
> > armed with cruel hate,
> On earth is not his equal.

Look at the profound Bible truths that come through in the second verse:

> Did we in our own strength confide,
> >   our striving would be losing,
> Were not the right Man on our side,
> >   the Man of God's own choosing.
> Dost ask who that may be?
> >   Christ Jesus, it is He.
> The Lord of hosts His name, from
> >   age to age the same,
> And He must win the battle.

Even when translated from German to English, this hymn is full of potent theology that communicates life-changing truths. It uplifts Christ, "the right Man on our side" and "the Man of God's own choosing." We are powerless "in our own strength" to fight "our ancient foe," the devil. It is Jesus who will "win the battle." The structure of the hymn is as deep as the theology it teaches. There are no two verses alike. It's like a full sermon that teaches relevant truths, especially meaningful to those who suffered during the Protestant Reformation under the established church.

A friend of mine wrote down the chords to this hymn so that I could play it on the guitar. Talk about a challenging piece! Done correctly, virtually every word requires a different note or chord, which means you change chords almost 40 times in each stanza—a real workout for your hand!

Many great Protestants wrote hymns that set forth the truths of the Bible, including John Newton, Isaac Watts, William Cowper, and Charles Wesley. The message of the Reformation exploded in large part because leaders like these were putting God's precious truths to music, establishing believers in sound doctrine.

Rich Lyrics Teach Truth

A 2001 study by two psychologists at the University of Leicester in the United Kingdom revealed that cows who listened to slow, soothing songs like Beethoven's Symphony No. 6, known also as the "Pastoral Symphony," or "Bridge Over

Troubled Water" by Simon & Garfunkel produced 3 percent more milk than a control group. In contrast, cows that listened to rap and techno music showed no increase in milk production.[31] Research has shown that oxytocin is crucial for a cow to produce milk and that the hormone is produced less when the animal is stressed. Thus, it certainly follows that playing a type of music which relaxes a cow would cause it to produce more oxytocin and, consequently, more milk.

What does sacred music produce more of? I've found a profound depth of theology in the lyrics of many of the old hymns; they are melodious tutors sent to lift up the eternal truths of Scripture.

When you study older hymns, you'll often notice more verses than what you typically find in today's popular Christian music. Newer hymnals even cut out verses, probably to squeeze more hymns into the volume. But at what cost?

Much of contemporary Christian music is full of sweet but shallow platitudes that present a happy-go-lucky, bubblegum Christianity. The basic theme is, "Find a happy thought and repeat it ten times." Admittedly, I do enjoy many of those praise songs, and there's an appropriate place for them. However, there's a definite trend that focuses on personal feelings instead of directing our minds to glorify God and His Word. Good feelings and true faith do not always flow in the same direction.

It takes a lot of thought to write a hymn that shares hope, inspires courage, and admonishes, comforts, and teaches by the Bible's doctrinal truths—and still have music that matches the message. And those kinds of hymns *produce* thought as well, provoking sharp, complex mental pictures. When you sing such hymns, you sing intelligently, with reason and purpose, not in a mindless and meandering way.

Music that hijacks our emotions so that we are not thinking rationally is not godly music. I believe that when we sing to the Lord, we should sing with both sides of our brain—the right side with emotion and the left side with our reasoning: "I will sing with the spirit, and I will also sing with the understanding"

(1 Corinthians 14:15). David said, "I will praise You, O Lord, with my whole heart" (Psalm 9:1). In Scripture, the heart and mind are used interchangeably: "I will put My laws in their mind and write them on their hearts" (Hebrews 8:10), said the Lord; "thus my heart was grieved, and I was vexed in my mind" (Psalm 73:21), said the psalmist. When we worship God in song, we shouldn't check our brains at the door.

Music with Depth

My mother was a successful and respected songwriter. She wrote pieces that were recorded by some well-known artists and worked with award-winning composers on Broadway. At one time, she assisted Sherman Edwards with the lyrics for *1776*, the Tony Award-winning musical about America's founding document, the Declaration of Independence. Edwards, a former history teacher, spent 10 years working on the numbers. When he hit a wall and could not get the words right, he'd recruit my mom to help. Sometimes, they'd spend a whole day working over just one song. Talk about a history lesson!

It was inspiring to watch them collaborate. Peter Stone, who wrote the musical's book, reportedly said, "There's more information about the Continental Congress in [its] opening song than I learned in all my years at school."[32]

In Matthew 6:7, Jesus said that we should avoid "vain repetition" in our praying; I think that principal applies to music as well. Some songs feel as if the composer ran out of ideas and just repeated certain phrases over and over.

Just to clarify: I am not against repetition in lyrics. Some repetition is good; repetition deepens impression, after all. For instance, we know angels and the four living creatures around the throne of God sing "Holy, holy, holy" (Isaiah 6:3; Revelation 4:8). And the psalms have repeated phrases, though I would add that very few of David's psalms are noted for repetition. Psalm 118 repeats the phrase "His mercy endures forever" five times—four times in just the first four verses. But then it covers other truths for 20 more verses before returning to its starting theme.

And look at Psalm 136—it repeats that same phrase even more. But notice how the repeated phrase is positioned to lead us in a faith-affirming direction. It reminds me of an anecdote I read in a commentary on the psalms by James Montgomery Boice. He writes:

> A number of years ago when my middle daughter, Heather, was just a teenager, she asked me one day if I thought her music was loud and repetitive. I sensed that I was being set up, but I replied that, Yes, I did think most of it was loud and repetitive, to which she responded, "Please explain the 'Hallelujah Chorus.'"
>
> After I had told that story once, one of our [church] musicians explained to me that the "Hallelujah Chorus" is not really repetitious. It advances musically toward its climax.[33]

There is a time and place for repetition as long as it serves a godly purpose—such as trying to guide our hearts toward heavenly truth.

But I'm concerned when music is *overly* repetitious with little depth of thought, almost like a hypnotizing Eastern or New Age chant. I used to be in the New Age movement before I became a Christian; I know what it sounds like. And I've heard contemporary Christian praise songs with a similar repetition.

Indeed, in recent years, the derogatory term "7-11 song" has cropped up in many a Christian circle. Essentially, it is a praise song that is composed of seven words sung 11 times in a row—quite a departure from the hymns of old.

Karen and I once visited China and heard Buddhist monks chanting with such monotony that it was spellbinding. I think almost every culture of the world has a form of this type of music. Are these 7-11 songs done to get the same mesmerizing effect? According to some, they are produced to do just that; in fact, it's all part of the "worship experience."[34]

Do you know another reason 7-11 songs were named that way? No offense to 7-Eleven, but the convenience store giant was not created to specialize in healthy foods, like fresh fruits, vegetables, and whole grains. Instead, they focus on coffee, doughnuts, candy, chips, snacks, sticky-sweet beverages, and other fast foods that people in a hurry grab and go. That's why convenience stores can charge such high prices, because they're convenient and in high demand. You could survive for a time on food from one of these quick-stop stores, but your doctor might have something to say at your next checkup.

A lot of contemporary Christian music is like getting low-quality food from a convenience store. They have some sweet melodies with lyrics that aren't bad, but I wouldn't suggest you live on a diet of these songs. They represent only one type of the many different styles of music that can bless your Christian walk.

If all of your music is like the quick foods you grab at a convenience store, you're going to end up with a malnourished church, which is the primary diet of a lot of churches today: a sliver of gospel truth for an exorbitant cost. We need less fast-food music and more nourishing songs with strong theological footings.

Fanny Crosby was a noted blind composer who wrote more than 8,000 hymns in her lifetime, some in a matter of minutes. She had a penchant for memorizing the Bible and for writing poetry. Her sole objective for writing hymns was to reach people for Christ; and before every hymn she composed, she would pray to God for guidance. Many of her hymns we still sing today, "Blessed Assurance" being among the most famous.[35] What would the music in our church be like if a hymnist like Fanny Crosby were alive today?

Do Different Cultures Have Different Musical Principles?

I've traveled around the world, and listening to the music in all these different cultures convinces me more than ever that the devil's same tactics are at work, no matter what continent you're on, no matter what language you speak, no matter what traditions you hold. Different instruments and rhythms might be used in various places, but the principles of music still hold true. Yes—culture plays a role in the flavors of music, but the guidelines of Scripture transcend culture.

Do you think Satan would set up boundaries in some countries of the world and not others? No, his work can be found everywhere. I once traveled to a country with a culture far different than North America's. When I was picked up by a couple of church members and taken to the place where I was to stay, the driver popped in a CD of supposedly Christian music. Yet even though I couldn't understand a word of what was played, it was far from heavenly music.

Should we be surprised that the devil will use music in the last days to lead people astray? Carefully consider this insightful counsel from a Christian writer—and focus on the principles, not the instruments, discussed:

The Lord has shown me [what] would take place just before the close of probation. Every uncouth thing will be demonstrated. There will be shouting, with drums, music, and dancing. The senses of rational beings will become so confused they cannot be trusted to make right decisions. And this is called the moving of the Holy Spirit.[36]

You might be shocked to learn that this prediction was written more than a hundred years ago. It is not describing what will take place in bars and clubs—but in churches. There is no question that we find this very state of frenzied ecstasy happening in many churches today in countries around the world.

This is what happened to Israel at Mount Sinai. While waiting 40 days for Moses to return from the mountain, the Israelites began to lose faith and compromise their convictions. Eventually, they conducted a wild worship service honoring a golden calf. Meanwhile, back up the mountain, Joshua told Moses he thought he heard the "noise of war in the camp" (Exodus 32:17). Interesting. Their worship music sounded like the bloodthirsty strains of battle, and it reached such a volume that it was heard even on the mountain.

Once more, there is nothing wrong with rejoicing loudly in the Lord, but loudness mixed with licentiousness is typically characteristic of chaos. I might add that under the influence of that counterfeit worship music, the Israelites compromised and broke virtually every commandment until "the people were naked" (v. 25 KJV). The Bible shows us that music has a direct connection to a church's moral direction.

I might briefly add here that a number of these issues spring from the problem that very few churches can afford to have full-time music ministers, singers, and players trained in the nuances of biblical music. Kings Solomon and Hezekiah recognized the importance of this position as a full-time job: "These are the singers … who lodged in the chambers, and were free from other duties; for they were employed in that work day and night" (1 Chronicles 9:33). For most churches, which typically have fewer than 100 members, you need to pray for a gifted volunteer to assist in leading the congregation in appropriate worship music.

What About Psalm 150?

Some quote Psalm 150 as an argument for incorporating syncopated drums and dancing in the church sanctuary:

> Praise the Lord!
> Praise God in His sanctuary;
> Praise Him in His mighty firmament!
> Praise Him for His mighty acts;
> Praise Him according to His
>   excellent greatness!
> Praise Him with the sound of the trumpet;
> Praise Him with the lute and harp!
> Praise Him with the timbrel and dance;
> Praise Him with stringed
>   instruments and flutes!
> Praise Him with loud cymbals;
> Praise Him with clashing cymbals!
> Let everything that has breath praise the Lord.
> Praise the Lord!

But a surface-level reading of this psalm may overlook some key points that have to do with context and culture. It's often been said about the Bible, "A text without its context becomes pretext."

First, this psalm was not performed inside the sanctuary. Its singers were not praising God from within a church but instead were directing their praise to God, who was *in His sanctuary* above and of which the earthly sanctuary was just a miniature version (Hebrews 8:2; 9:1, 24). This is why the next verse says "in His mighty firmament."

Second, the children of Israel never walked into the earthly sanctuary with clashing cymbals; neither did they dance in it. In fact, the common Israelite never went into the earthly structure at all (Numbers 18:22, 23), of which there were two compartments, the Holy Place and the Most Holy Place. Only the priests went into the Holy Place (Exodus 28–30), and only the high priest went into the Most Holy Place once a year (Leviticus 16).

Thus, we can know that Psalm 150 has nothing to do with music during a worship service. In fact, it falls more into the category of a joyous celebration, as when David led the ark of the covenant toward Jerusalem (2 Samuel 6:5, 14), or a victory parade, such as when the Israelites were returning from a triumphant battle. The women would come out to meet them on the road, singing, playing timbrels, and dancing for joy. (See Exodus 15:20, 21; Judges 11:34; 1 Samuel 18:6, 7.)

On a side note, the dancing done by the Hebrews was also completely different from the modern dances of today. These victory dances did not pair off men and women, as we see at parties or nightclubs; they weren't sensual dances like the one Salome performed for King Herod and his guests, after which she asked for the head of John the Baptist.

Using Psalm 150 to define what kind of music, instruments, and worship styles should be used in a church sanctuary is inaccurate and fallacious. One might perhaps be more curious as to why certain people want to push a particular preference for a certain type of music in the church. Should we not instead humbly and diligently search God's Word for the manner in which He desires to be worshiped? (Acts 17:11).

Conclusion

Just as Christians need to constantly screen the books we read, the videos we watch, the thoughts we think, so we must prayerfully evaluate our music, both what we consume and what we put out. Is it nurturing the spirit—or is it troubling the flesh?

I love music, and it is an integral part of the Christian experience, whether one is hearing inspiring orchestral music, or participating in energetic congregational singing, or quietly playing a spiritual song in one's own room. Because it is such an important piece of our walk with God, I share these thoughts to encourage you in making wise choices.

In this little volume, I've attempted to focus on a balanced approach to music and the Christian by looking at Bible principles. The Scriptures not only reveal the power of music on the mind and heart but also the struggle between good and evil in the context of music that is happening right now in our current world. These are principles that you can count on, beyond culture and beyond time. They can be used or abused. The choice, as always, is yours.

And keep in mind, even the best Christian music in the world is little more than a discordant cacophony compared with the angelic orchestras in heaven:

> There will be music there, and song, such music and song as, save in the visions of God, no mortal ear has heard or mind conceived. "As well the singers as the players on instruments shall be there." "They shall lift up their voice, they shall sing for the majesty of the Lord." "For the Lord shall comfort Zion: … He will make her wilderness like Eden, and her desert like the garden of the Lord: joy and gladness shall be found therein, thanksgiving, and the voice of melody."[37]

I pray that the music choices you make will always be guided by Scripture and prepare you to someday stand on the sea of glass with the redeemed, "[singing] the song of Moses, the servant of God, and the song of the Lamb, saying: 'Great and marvelous are Your works, Lord God Almighty! Just and true are Your ways, O King of the saints!'" (Revelation 15:3).

Endnotes

1. https://www.myplainview.com/news/article/Killer-who-claimed-influence-by-rap-music-executed-8513393.php
2. https://www.pbs.org/weta/washingtonweek/blog-post/16-things-know-about-ben-carson
3. https://thefederalist.com/2019/08/28/secretary-ben-carson-says-he-didnt-know-brain-surgery-was-supposed-to-be-stressful
4. https://greatergood.berkeley.edu/article/item/how_many_emotions_can_music_make_you_feel
5. https://www.wearethemighty.com/mighty-history/listen-to-the-tango-the-red-army-used-to-intimidate-the-nazis-at-stalingrad/
6. https://www.theguardian.com/books/2017/may/16/the-science-of-songs-how-does-music-effect-your-body-chemistry
7. https://www.toolshero.com/communication-skills/communication-model-mehrabian/
8. https://www.health.harvard.edu/staying-healthy/music-and-health
9. https://www.thelancet.com/journals/lancet/article/PIIS0140-6736(15)60169-6/fulltext
10. https://www.scientificamerican.com/article/music-therapy-heart-cardiovascular/

11. https://voices.no/index.php/voices/article/view/2308/2063
12. https://www.tandfonline.com/doi/abs/10.1080/17439760.2012.747000
13. https://www.sciencedaily.com/releases/2013/05/130514185336.htm
14. http://www.musicianbrain.com/papers/Norton_MelodicIntonationTherapy_nyas_04859.pdf
15. https://blog.sonicbids.com/5-facts-about-music-and-the-brain
16. https://www.mirror.co.uk/news/weird-news/britney-spears-music-blasted-out-2646660
17. E. G. White, Education, (Mountain View, CA: Pacific Press Publishing Association, 1903), 168.
18. https://www.hopkinsmedicine.org/health/wellness-and-prevention/keep-your-brain-young-with-music
19. Ronald W. Holz, "The Story Behind Salvation Army Music," Christian History, 1990, https://christianhistoryinstitute.org/magazine/article/story-behind-salvation-army-music.
20. https://www.hymnologyarchive.com/johnson-oatman-jr
21. https://www.smithsonianmag.com/arts-culture/phonograph-changed-music-forever-180957677/

22 Wilhelmina Dunbar, "The Human Voice: God's Precious Gift," Adventist World, August 9, 2014, 15.
23 https://www.christianitytoday.com/history/2008/august/when-did-churches-start-using-instrumental-music.html
24 http://www.classichistory.net/archives/organ
25 https://www.statista.com/statistics/310746/share-music-album-sales-us-genre/
26 https://www.bbc.com/news/health-31661789
27 https://murfreesborohearing.com/how-hearing-works
28 Aeneas Sylvius, History of Bohemia, 54, quoted in J. A. Wylie, The History of Protestantism, vol. 1 (London: Cassell, Petter & Galpin, 1878), 164.
29 E. G. White, "The Light of the World," Signs of the Times, Oct. 20, 1887, 625.
30 https://factsandtrends.net/2016/12/30/sound-theology-teaching-your-people-through-music/
31 http://news.bbc.co.uk/2/hi/science/nature/1408434.stm
32 https://www.mentalfloss.com/article/65795/10-star-spangled-facts-about-musical-1776
33 James Montgomery Boice, Psalms 107–150: An Expositional Commentary (Grand Rapids, MI: Baker Books, 2005), 1286, 1287.

34 https://www.dictionaryofchristianese.com/7-11-song/
35 https://www.christianitytoday.com/history/people/poets/fanny-crosby.html
36 E. G. White, Selected Messages, vol. 2 (Washington, D.C.: Review and Herald Publishing Association, 1958), 36.
37 E. G. White, Maranatha (Washington, D.C.: Review and Herald Publishing Association, 1976), 361.

If you enjoyed this book you'll love these DVDs ..

Kingdoms in Time
DV-KITSE

The Final Events of
Bible Prophecy
DV-FENC

Cosmic Conflict
DV-CCS

Revelation: The Bride, the
Beast & Babylon
DV-RBBBS

Amazing Health Facts
DV-AHFSE

Lake of Fire
DV-LOF

AFBookstore.com | 800-538-7275
*Bulk pricing available

WANT TO LEARN MORE?

Discover life-changing Bible truth in these colorful magazines from Amazing Facts!

The Day of the Lord
BK-DOTL

The Final Events of Bible Prophecy
BK-FE

Daniel and Revelation
BK-DRM

A Divine Design
BK-DDJT

Amazing Health Facts!
BK-AHF

Hidden Truth
BK-HT

The Afterlife Mystery
BK-ALM

America in Bible Prophecy
BK-AIP

AFBookstore.com | 800-538-7275
*Bulk pricing available

Did you love this book?

Find more great Christian resources—from books and magazines to DVDs and sharing resources—that will grow your faith and help you become a more informed and confident Christian!

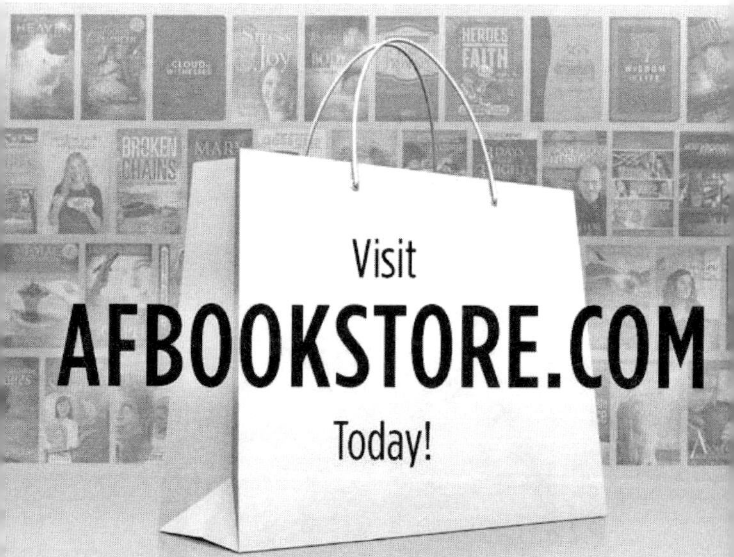

Visit
AFBOOKSTORE.COM
Today!

Get Bible Truth in Your Pocket!

The New Amazing Facts Mobile App

The Amazing Facts App puts our best resources into your hands—ready to inform you and help you share the good news with others no matter where you go!

Features ...

- AFTV
- *Sabbath School Study Hour*
- *Amazing Facts with Doug Batchelor*
- *Bible Answers Live*
- 24/7 Internet Radio
- Free Book Library
- Plus, Study Guides, Weekly Blog, and more!

Available now for iOS and Android

▶ **DOWNLOAD TODAY!**

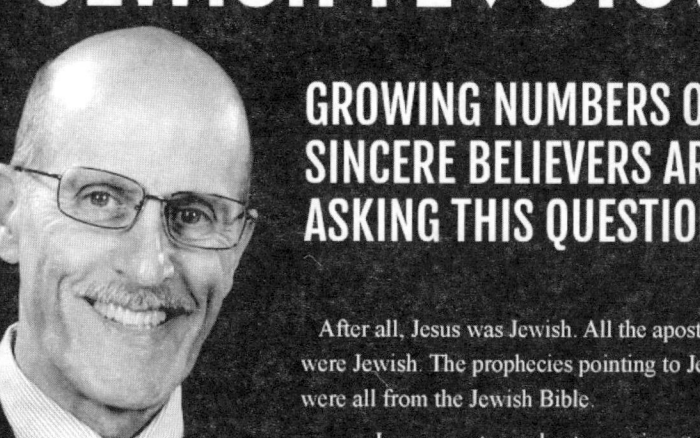

Find Peace, Power, and Purpose for YOUR LIFE!

amazingfacts.org

Enroll in our FREE online Bible study course and discover:

- What happens after death
- The way to better health
- How to save your marriage
- The surprising news about hell
- Why the Bible is relevant today
- The "mark of the beast"
- Who really gets "left behind"
- ... and much more!

Or enroll in the **FREE** postal mail course! Send your name and address to:

P.O. Box 909
Roseville, CA 95678